MW00785557

Guided Grief

Remembrance Journal

A Handbook and Keepsake To Help You Heal

With Joyous Memories

Written By: Lauren Stephan Cohen

Drawings by: Emma Caroline Rhoads

Copyright © 2019

ISBN 978-0-578-57497-4

Made in the USA

DEDICATION

This book is dedicated to my mother, Susie Stephan, who passed from Lymphoma & Leukemia on June 5, 2017.

She was the best mother I could ever ask for, and I am so grateful that I was gifted her as my mother. My life will never be the same without her. Even though she was taken from this Earth too soon, I am so thankful that I had 30 years being cared for, loved by, and best friends with such a wonderful woman.

I am the woman I am today because of her impeccable guidance and love. I know that one day we will meet again on the other side, and until then, I will cherish all of the joyful memories we had together.

PREFACE

I created this journal to help guide you through happy memories of a loved one who has passed. I decided to write this book so that I could easily share the wonderful memories I have of my mother with my future children and loved ones, and so I could have an uplifting tool to reference when I'm feeling sad that she has crossed to the other side. I use it as part of my healing and gratitude practice to remind myself of how lucky I was to have such an amazing mother.

I often find myself, in these early stages of grief, being flooded with the images of her illness and death more than the special memories I have of her for the first 30 years of my life. As many people know who have lost a love one, it's natural to experience the sad and painful memories and emotions surrounding the death. I have a separate journal for documenting all of the emotions that come with my grief. As I worked through my grief, I was most comforted by the many positive memories: the laughs, the smiles, the hugs, the lessons learned, and the love.

I wanted a way to memorialize and share the special, positive emotions with those who loved my mother and those who would have if they had a chance to meet her. This guided journal is intended specifically for the uplifting memories, to remind us of the profound, positive impact our loves ones had on us, and to serve as an inspiration for family and generations to come. I believe that their family and friends have a duty and obligation to celebrate their life and the impact they had on us as much as possible.

There are pages in this book that are left with blank space by design so you can, if you'd like, add photos of your loved one, pictures of things that remind you of them, draw, paint, color, add stickers, whatever your heart desires. Don't put pressure on yourself to complete this book in one sitting. You can take as much or as little time as you want on this. Let it be a therapeutic and creative tool for you whenever you need it. Write more memories in it whenever they come to mind. This will be a keepsake to comfort you that you will have forever.

I hope that this journal helps you like it has helped me!

This book is dedicated to happy memories of

....

My favorite memories of them are...

....

....

....

....

....

....

....

....

....

....

....

....

....

....

....

They always brought a smile to my face when...

11

Places that bring back fond memories of them are...

....

....

....

....

....

....

....

....

....

....

....

....

....

....

....

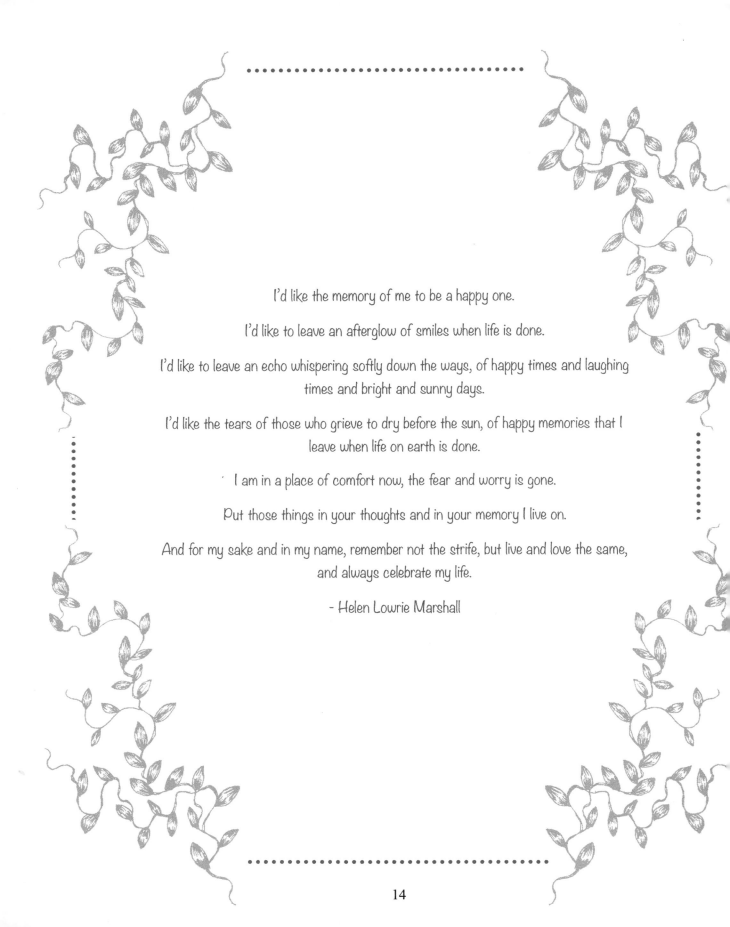

I'd like the memory of me to be a happy one.

I'd like to leave an afterglow of smiles when life is done.

I'd like to leave an echo whispering softly down the ways, of happy times and laughing times and bright and sunny days.

I'd like the tears of those who grieve to dry before the sun, of happy memories that I leave when life on earth is done.

I am in a place of comfort now, the fear and worry is gone.

Put those things in your thoughts and in your memory I live on.

And for my sake and in my name, remember not the strife, but live and love the same, and always celebrate my life.

- Helen Lowrie Marshall

Words to describe them are...

....

....

....

....

....

....

....

....

....

....

....

....

....

....

....

Things everybody loved about them are...

....

....

....

....

....

....

....

....

....

....

....

....

....

....

....

Things we loved to do together are...

Imagine if I was given one moment, just a single slice of my past.
I could hold it close forever, and that moment would always last.

I'd put the moment in a safe, within my heart's abode.
I could open it when I wanted, and only I would know the code.

I could choose a time of laughing, a time of happiness and fun.
I could choose a time that tried me through everything I've done.

I sat and thought about what moment would always make me smile.
One that would always push me to walk that extra mile.

If I'm feeling sad and low, if I'm struggling with what to do,
I can go and open my little safe and watch my moment through.

There are moments I can think of that would lift my spirits every time.
The moments when you picked me up, when the road was hard to climb.

For me to only pick one moment to cherish, save and keep
is proving really difficult, as I've gathered up a heap!

I've dug deep inside my heart, found the safe and looked inside
There was room for lots of moments; in fact, hundreds if I tried.

I'm building my own little library, embedded in my heart,
for all the moments spent with you before you had to part.

I can open it up whenever I like, pick a moment and watch it through,
My little library acts as a promise I'll never ever forget you.

- Sarah Blackstone

Their favorite things to do were...

Favorite memories from holidays, celebrations, events, and traditions are...

....

....

....

....

....

....

....

....

....

....

....

....

....

....

I admired them for...

....

....

....

....

....

....

....

....

....

....

....

....

....

....

....

....

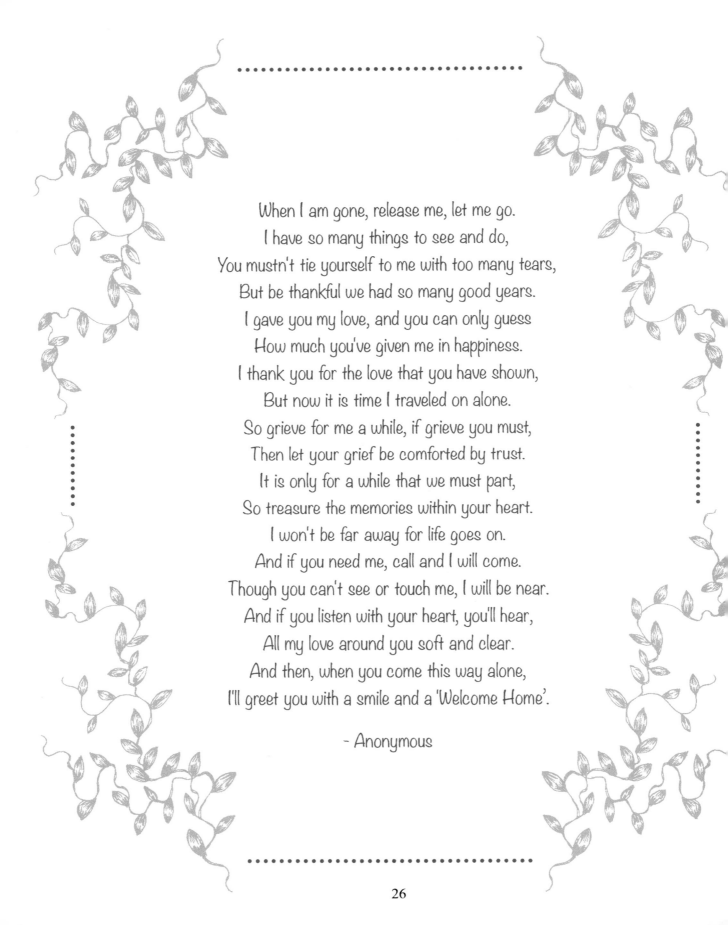

When I am gone, release me, let me go.
I have so many things to see and do,
You mustn't tie yourself to me with too many tears,
But be thankful we had so many good years.
I gave you my love, and you can only guess
How much you've given me in happiness.
I thank you for the love that you have shown,
But now it is time I traveled on alone.
So grieve for me a while, if grieve you must,
Then let your grief be comforted by trust.
It is only for a while that we must part,
So treasure the memories within your heart.
I won't be far away for life goes on.
And if you need me, call and I will come.
Though you can't see or touch me, I will be near.
And if you listen with your heart, you'll hear,
All my love around you soft and clear.
And then, when you come this way alone,
I'll greet you with a smile and a 'Welcome Home'.

- Anonymous

I will always cherish the times when...

I am proud of them for...

....

....

....

....

....

....

....

....

....

....

....

....

....

....

....

The lessons I learned from them are...

I know that no matter what
You will always be with me.
When life separates us
I'll know it is only your soul
Saying goodbye to your body
But your spirit will be with me always.
When I see a bird chirping on a nearby branch
I will know it is you singing to me.
When a butterfly brushes gently by me
I will know it is you assuring me you are free from pain.
When the gentle fragrance of a flower catches my attention
I will know it is you reminding me
To appreciate the simple things in life.
When the sun shining through my window awakens me
I will feel the warmth of your love.
When I hear the rain pitter patter against my window sill
I will hear your words of wisdom
And will remember what you taught me so well
That without rain trees cannot grow
Without rain flowers cannot bloom
Without life's challenges I cannot grow strong.
No matter where I am
Your spirit will be beside me
For I know that no matter what
You will always be with me.

- Tram-Tiara T. Von Reichenbach

The signs, images, songs, scents, foods, and more that remind me of them are...

....

....

....

....

....

....

....

....

....

....

....

....

....